NEW ENGLAND SUITE

NEW ENGLAND SUITE

Selected Poems, 1950–1962

By Charles Philbrick

Clarke & Way, Inc., New York

Some of these poems have been published by the following magazines:

APPROACH
ARBOR
THE BELOIT POETRY JOURNAL
THE COLORADO QUARTERLY
FIDDLEHEAD (Canada)
HAWK AND WHIPPOORWILL
INLAND
INSCAPE
MUTINY
THE NATION
THE NEW MEXICO QUARTERLY
THE RHODE ISLAND SCHOOL OF DESIGN ALUMNI BULLETIN
SATURDAY REVIEW
THE SEWANEE REVIEW
VIEWS
VOICES
THE WESTERN HUMANITIES REVIEW

To the Memory of my Father

TABLE OF CONTENTS

I

NEW ENGLAND SUITE

1.

I hear in my brain all New England echoing down and around me,
And in the colony of my heart away. My land is a factory now,
Or a suburb, a parking-lot liquid in sun on the levelling asphalt,
Below local histories, markers and chartered ground, beneath brick,
Bright cemented disclaimers, lies crushed and still Indian-
Haunted rock, lie the bones of hard people often uncomely and cold,
Lie swatches of hair, and commodes, lie mirrors and lobster-pots, letters
In palimpsest, arrowheads, fish-knives, and ropes now all mummied in tar;
Good families books and chipped jugs, penwipers, samplers and useful shells;
Whalebones and beads, genealogy, sweetgrass and old uphill passions;
Birchbark and dimity, cracked leather straps and shrunk iron, denials;
And spyglasses empty of eye, the salted-green brassbound recallers
Of the masted-in-intricate-pride, of the widowing seas, and the land
Sea defines: the tides of the mind leave this wrack on the memory's shore.

2.

The regional bird is the gull, protected by law, protecting
And proctoring, fouling and scavenging all our most visited shores:
Able, unlovely, raucous, persistent, at home in the storm;
Friendless, eternal, yellow of eye and whitely aware;
Undiscouraged if dun, a clown to the camera, famishers' food.
The southering bird on whose feather has fallen the rumor of snow,
The flier afflicted with instinct and warned by the touch and the go
Of a soft geometric—that sniff and that sift in the needling air—
He leaves. All the birds know by the cold, and believe in the sun,
Slant as he may.

        (And you watch. When last did a bird of this world
Seize a child from your bloody town, mar a woman, accuse or unmake
Any man?)

        To the birds who ensky many myths they would scorn—

Who high-bracket New England—New England is only a flat like a
    map,
With the waters precise in the infinite inlets, a visible ground
Laid out for their feeding, is neither to nest on nor haply to fall.
For themselves, the seen birds, whether migrants or natives, have
    never
Been known to give names to the curious people, to count and report
All the tourists or label the ankles of strangers like herons who stalk
The emptying estuaries, quiet, with glass to the questing eye.

3.

Musselled, sea-lavendered shores throwing beaches, low dikes
To put sand between salt of the wave and the salt of the meadowing
    marshes
Where silt waves have grained into grasses of silver and green, are
    unpeopled
Like the beaches that run under gull-foot, below eagled cliffs and the
    headlands
Inspected by whales, or the uplands patrolled by the bear overhill
And the horsy, high-shouldered moose with antlers of ossified kelp.
From mountain to shore, through hills, rises, valleys and rivers, odd
    ponds
In their pockets, the bent stands of scrub and the hungry foundations,
    all acres,
The regional beast is no proudfoot, deep in his chest, nor a brightmane;
No flasher of eyes, nor bayonet-brandisher frightful of man;
The regional beast is a trinity noxious to dogs, knowing men:
The muskrat, the skunk and the woodchuck, all drab in defiance,
    all near.

4.

The regional fish is the mackerel, or else the low pastoral cod
In the market; but over the eyelid's horizon goes swimming away,
Like a barrel of anguish, the great whale trailing his stintless blood
In a moonpath of red across the Pacific savannas, and huge
Green valleys down, below the white sails and crisp oars,
The sharp intentions, going under and down. Both whaler and whale,
Pursuit and profit, loss and return of the voyagers, now
Read as history's blow; and the strike and the flurry, the sounding,
The flensing, the reek of the try-out recede to a region
Of rowboats for rent and of dories agap and awash with petunias,
Of seafood at roadside, clean restrooms and gas. The regional fish
Is the clamcake announced in electrical script; the seasonal fish
Is the sucker.
          And all New England echoes down and away.

          5.

Violet, daisy, sweet-william and blackeyed susan, sea-rose,
Queen-anne's-lace, the goldenrod, sumac and orient hydrangea
Unbelieved, but brought home by new-bearded son with new judgment
     in eyes—
Like lilac, no bride was declared in the cargo; columbine, laurel
And honeysuckle, trumpet-vine, buttercup—all these combine
To make the regional flower: with fireweed and Indian-pipe,
     paint-brush
Of devils, the gentian, the jewelweed, milkweed, the poison-bright ivy:
These, and more, are given to see. The good herbs are left to discover.
The flowers were pressed between leaves of the books—the few
     books and good—
And the books were impressed on the brains; on a continent brains
     were then sown.

6.

Whole graveyards on hillsides are stone-fledged with beards up-ended
To heaven and frozen at chin to the flint of the soil; whole hillsides
Are graveyards unhallowed, perimeters nubile with birches like hopes
Of young serious virgins, all clean and surrounded by sentinel cedars:
Dark daggers at wrong, evergreen like original sin. Planted here
In this undulant underground churchyard, are the hopes of
    New England,
Unique in their angles and white in their morals, unique in their bite
On the sky; these fears are redeemed by their force, which made
    and still makes
But metaphor of winter weather. The wind frays the flags and shrivels
The wreaths that sag onto urns eroded, under stiff wings
In the moving air over earth of such coffined rectitude,
Cold regard of recording stones, generations of marbled woe.

7.

Our tree is ubiquitous pine—possibly spruce or the tamarack,
Maple whose blood bespeaks sugar in veins—but the bark is of birch,
And the leaf is the loyal hard brown old man's hand of the oak.
Sweet groundpine or juniper, wild grape or bayberry, brambles—
    all run
Like the nerves of this ground whose berries taste tart as an apothegm.
But the tree that the colonists planted as badge of their towns
    was another—
And this is their reason: the reach and the slendering height of
    the straight,
Academic, imperious elm, like the aim of New England in art,
Lurks in the crook of the root gripping soil, in its thirst among rocks.

8.

The regional colors are wilder by contrast and subtler than Mexico.
The urge of the autumn, the accent of frost, makes the primary chords:
The scarlets and oranges, yellows and purples, the high exclamations
In leaf, and the firmer, full statements in fruit. Brown earth and
      pale sand,
And impossible snow make the canvas. The sky and the sea do the rest:
All the blue, gray and silver, all greens not alive that can change;
All the changes among them, and sunsets in season, all weathering
      motions.
The regional hues that are minor are man's: the glosses of lanterns
And tar, the dulled ictus of rust and the glint of the hair-thin ring,
Wedding-gold.
          The regional colors dream under neon, and wait.

9.

The life of New England in centuries gone is a guess, or proverbial guff.
Lust could wear homespun and wonder on calico, sun sweeten sweat
On the skin, or skin get the alternate ache of dry salt from the sea;
Love could walk barefoot and brown with the dust of the sun,
      or go booted,
And berried in cheek and bright lip by the hollying frost. The life
Of the regional youth was no glimpse between headstones of
      wives early gone
From the childbed and footstones of children stillborn or
      but shown for a season
Or two. The life of the youth of this country was not just a summer
Following thaw, before blizzard, a sun between snows. The youth
Of this region was everything strong, little easy: if hard, yet it shone.

—Cleaning and bleaching, mending and patching, painting with paint,
Oil or varnish, with whitewash or tar; the quilting and candling,
    preserving
And saving, here making and there making do—but they made!
    To mend
Is a form of *to make*, and to paint is a shaping, an outward approval;
Doing without is an aspect of using: the use of each thing is to wear
It utterly out, as loving old couples have done of their bodies,
Yet live and apparently love; as thinkers have whittled their brains
Into words, and still see things and laugh, as the poets I know
From this region can go to the antarctic ice-cap, alone with a pen,
And there make New England of nothing, or scrimshaw whole
    Indies of ice.

    10.
*These states are my mind, and my blood with their history flows all down
And away, bleeding west in an empire and south in a passion; these states
Are the map of my intricate heart, and no orderly page and no print
Can reduce them to handbook. The mind flows away to beginnings in water,
Past sand, over rocks and rock-pools, to the rising of hills through the pines
And the pine-heavy air of all lands, and across the whole cloud of the sky.
Yet my mind is this country of slower than tropical, longer, more passionate
Growth, and this ocean contains my imaginings; mountains suggest
My haphazard projects; astonishing snows are my silences, gales
My level declaring of autumn. In August untended wild roses
That overwhelm silvering shingles of cedar amount to my tenderness.
Quite like a monument, steepled and peeling of paint, worth preserving
By the civic of mind, I am nothing alone without gift of this ground
To grow in and give in the double-bed dark to my boys in the sacrament
Love before driving the seed of my being, long warm with a wife
And all green with a poem, under the quilt of this eldering earth.*

II

FIVE AGES OF ART

1.

When I stretched alone in the cool gloom of our cave
In the pinnacles of the green Sahara, to score with fear
On the virgin wall the spirit-lines of the antelope
Whose liquid speed he drank from our waters and ate
From the curving reeds along our stream, who breathed
From our earth the colors we had slowly learned to dig,
The colors I would slowly, with old and fearful joy,
Corral in the line I made, when my flint brought it back
To the point on the tip of the horn at which it began—
When I did this, sweating like a god in the cool cave,
I did not know that I lived too soon for history, for time
Was not behind us; and I had no idea of where I would stand
In the progress of the arts, for I didn't know that the arts
Were so far apart from a man's life-work that they could change.

2.

When I crouched on the cooking sands of the Libyan desert
To study the broken chariot that cost us this loss to Them,
I was given a glimpse of a new design which would please
Both the gods and the commander: it seemed what the gods
Must have meant the old design to become, and it ought to be
Swifter in sand, more easily fixed out here, and would please
My secret heart by the cleaner line its carriage could take.
When I sweated this vision out of my vagrant mind in my owned
And sweat-clad body, I was happy that I might add this grain
To the glory of the empire which was already history's base,
And would be the peak of man's progress. That power and fear
Could sweep over peoples in handsomer cars was my fulfilment,
My tribute to the city, to which even slaves like me yearned
To go back, for no man wants a new master who's killed the old.

3.

When I paced my cell to get warm, and with the abbot's leave
Permitted my mind to wrestle with self for the glory of God,
I slaved to gloss the dark language of my dreams, to pierce
The images of nightmare, hang the devil high where he belongs.
I kept my hair below the tonsure long and tangled, so the lice
Would be harder to scratch away; and all my bathing was to spill
Icewater on the most descended parts of man, to freeze my breech.
I hoped that, with the Holy Spirit's help, and an older holy man
To guide me through the luring visions—as of skin-warmed silk
Over oil-soft hair, and the hot anathema that lurks within—
I could allegorize in my cold cell all curses from the fall,
And chronicle on our great scrolls each danger Satan can set
In the young man's path who seeks the eternal city; and hoped
That then they would let me illuminate the text of this *confessio*.

4.

Confession was core of my art; I told more secrets than I had,
And I let their acid shred the facades of a century. My verse
Ripped the robes off hypocrites, and sketched the very nerves
That drove and tortured the new man, alive to foul predicaments.
Prefaces poured from my pen, and my manifestoes entitled the age.
I diligently made my life a gold-field for apologists, my name
A flag for those free few who knew that nothing fathers taught
Was true, but all designed to fetter the dangerous spirit.
When I was slashed, and no longer snubbed, by all the most
Respected journals, I knew that I had reached the peak unseen;
And drew my disciples more tightly to me, bound them forever
Into my fame. I didn't know that my most radical proclamations,
As well as my midnight mysteries and programmatic love-affairs,
Would breed dissertations, footnotes. I would have changed nothing.

5.

When I had finished my doctoral essay, and hidden it safe
In the college library, I knew (as one knows when one is sick)
That I never could bring myself to be the publishing scholar.
So I began to print my impeccable poems, subtly aware of works
Which exercised my colleagues most that year. I wrote for them
And for the oldest little magazines our library took; and I began
Unawares to let my students guess that, when I talked of poetry,
I talked—inevitably—from the inside out: from life, not books.
I taught them to query footnotes, and to smile at earlier notions
Of voices from above, afflatus, gleams, alastors and furor poeticus;
I put my polite quietus on claims of inspiration. I led them up
To Poe, then left them there, suggesting a lexicon of rhymes
To buy, and a course or two to take in cultural anthropology.
I got myself promoted young, and shrugged my robes at history.

HINDSIGHT AND STONE

No matter how young or well-known you think you are,
How emptily praised and given X thousands of days,
If you're smart enough and an hour alone, you know
In your easiest chair that death has taken dead aim
At your loins, and you feel the squirm of inanition,
The clutch of impotence, no matter when.

Then you can stare at a fireplace, black and square,
Cold, and see beyond its screen and clean bricks
The oldest stones, whether shaped or placed,
Warmed by the first deliberate, domestic fire
In a much less comfortable cave, and set by a man
Whose feet are as hands, whose words only speak
In his eyes and shoulder-shrugs as he cooks
The meat that sliced his arms, when it was alive,
And that, smoking now, wets and thickens his tongue.

Seeing him crouched, full of seasons (millenia down),
Tending his future so seriously, close to the fire,
Lest the provender burn, unaware that he's naked,
Not seeing the firelight cavort on his cheekbones,
Or the urging and smelly, the utterly attractive
Ur-woman behind him, always at and on his side,
As he surlily cooks (it will strengthen them, hot) —
I apologize to the spirit of fire, and this first
Of its makers, that my kind inherits his life's long watch:

I of the lightswitch, I of the fabrics nice to my skin,
Wife sleeping safely in softness, up the sawn stairs,
I, stupid, delivered of hardship, of foraging ages,
I shudder all back to the chance-life, the finding,
The taking of food, the making of fire by my forefather,
Leaf-sheds of seasons ago, big cities of firesides away.

The flame of my getting dies down as my memories mount
All the steps of my growing, tread history, and hew
Newly the long-dug ground that contains him, awaits me,
If fate, late or soon, should award me such honor.
No matter how famous or fruitful, or little, I've lived,
As I'll die, on lives deeded through glory and pain;
May my shames be smothered by the gentlest of things
That work on this earth, both delicate and deep,
And no matter how long. That is good sleep.

ADAM ON THE HANGING MAN

Why was I made man's candidate,
God's bad design, zoologizing there?
I who labored dully as my bride
Went botanist upon a dream of a toad,
With worm around that one unneeded tree.

Spectrums of names fade off my tasted tongue:
That thick, original instrument with which
I should have asked blinding Michael license for
His sword; his God, for all the thunder dumped on us
In such a fenced and changeless place—and us to go

Like this to give the desert unangelic young,
In blood, near thorny springs, give genealogies.
Trees I have known, may know in my seed or song:
Even some three, cut, later, unleaved, fruitless trees.

A QUESTION OR TWO, IF YOU PLEASE, MR. MILTON:

How many times, before tooth entered knowledge,
Did One go into Two?
A into E equalled how many inches
Of innocent, leafless fun?
Were the beasts also sterile they named in the garden,
Or did that Original Birth Control
Come only to image, a gift like the soul?
Why, indeed, did the first deliverer rib
His patient, first born, with a sib?
Was it after he planted the glittering tree, and before
He drew out the well-languaged worm, or even
Compacted that forensic toad?
Did the figleaves flourish nearby through foreknowledge?
Had angels been tending the flames for the sword?
Was it simply to match the red skin of the apple
That E was fated the first thing to bleed?
And that fortunate fall, which engendered us all
(Although it disabled C),
Was it planned for the purpose of growing the thorn.
That abecedarian sin?

JOSEPH MUSING

The last part was there from nearly the start:
In the T-square and the skin-smooth tools
That slither to pierce the novice palm.

God, was there ever a man like me in my days?
Or a Man like mine?
                              All of it lives with me now . . .

(A swirl of hectoring Herod and leather-loined John,
The joiner, honey-mouthed with a gut full of locusts . . .
Cycles of circumstance . . . always the lurking wicked one,
Despite the hungred adolescent on the peak . . . new wine
Into new bottles, those figged thistles, rain on just
And unjust, ignorant left hand, and halo of the moths,
Rust corrupted out of sunlight, lending savor to
The spended salt, releasing Simon from his care
And Andrew from the mending nets . . . thou fool . . .
The threatened fire, and the uttermost farthing . . .
Leading them, doctoring all the way . . . adultery
Of hearts, and Hell's reiteration.) Well:

This was an issue of blood, a braid of bloods, a body
Bred for forty-two blood-tides up from Abraham.
From Abraham to Adam takes it back through all begats
To gates, dividing leaves, the sweet persuasion and the crisp
Participation in the apple, to the toad, the ribbing sleep,
The nomenclature, and the first commands young God
Decided to give Adam, first and youngest man, and angel last.

I? Should put her privily away? How? The Holy Ghost
Espoused her first, so young; the angel of the Lord
Gave seed and order, said to Joseph, said to me:
Marry her, fair damaged goods, untouched and deified;
After this issue all your knowledge comes, and none before.

What other spawn for her? What salty seed might spring
In human night, from the second coming first?
                                        The angel
Failed to say. Old Joseph's knowledge always must be late,
In exile, far from feathered call, the beasted birth—
Long before temptation in the scales or burden for the hill—
Before the rabbis of monstrosity could freeze the boy I raised
In that wide attitude of high defeat.
                                Legend, scriptured,
Leads to ladders in this way, to rungs of episode
In the long wrestle up to Heaven, where that Son sits bright
On the right hand of Omniscience, white, apart, alone
From me, with His own Mother later come to serve . . .
What carving now, of tool in wood, can rediscover Him?

What carving, ever in all the sawdust days to come,
Can rediscover me, the soiled man of wood whose Son
Attained and thus redeemed the Tree?
                                What will they see?
A primitive figurine, sexless, or my sex's oldest fool.

Elevated butt, neglected saint, the consort of the queen;
Virgin father whose sown bride was fated to inspire
Men denied, in wet cells to kneel by slimmest beds
And worship warm virginity that God put out of touch.

I was father forestalled by a stalled child, an ox among
Those mild of eye in the wild-starred night that drew
The watchers from their hills, three searchers from
Rich distance and another age, to look at what
We brought to Bethlehem for census and tax.

Mary, Jesus, Joseph—tortured trinity!
                                I'm more than old,

27

A carpenter who needed kings, and got one with a gift
Of tongues. The grooves of grain wormed to the floor,
Forgotten as they fell in curls:
                                        and scrolls so dry
To the trembling touch of history, recording, blunt, but this:
The site of the fatal rise, fatalities, imprimature and coin
Of that career-man, tested judge, cold-skilled
Administrator (What's his name?) of those obscure
And god-struck tribes I sprang from to this loneliness.

Robed in the flag they wave at my wife's child,
And claiming right from that boy's doom, the lords
Of rage may slay with satisfaction all the serfs
Of flesh, the tenants of their passing time, while I,
As Joseph, shall remain the world's protagonist
Of evirate uxoriousness, the patron saint of witnesses,
Man of my Mary's multiple sorrows, wanderer, wonderer
Among the stations of a councilled deity
And codified beliefs to be shaped in places far,
Far from there and then.
                                        How young he was when he
Took up the road to death—how old I am while I
Look down that road I did not climb—how lovely she
Was when we travelled tenderly, before we knew! O God,
How can they remember my short, my buried name?

His mouth I remember—the hair on his lips, the hair
That stroked the hands I trained in control of metal—
That moving mouth so easily painted and wrong, so long
Ago, and so right when the words were simple, mouth
So raised in monumental agony, and opened in the last,
The next-to-shout of all questions.
                                        He is gone,
As she is gone, and as I am going, to more than this,

To more than one man's memory, gone to great reward
Among the followers who really sired upon the centuries
That Son my dead wife bore, whose first cries Joseph, I,
Was first to hear alone.
                                    But I'm a carpenter whose hands
Are old, with even older wits to understand the things
They say and will say of that boy. I'll craft my simple box
Alone at last, unwitnessed in mistakes. And it may be
That later I shall know what really happened, and know why.

I married her and paid my tax; I'm Joseph, exile to the world.

VENUS GROWN OLD

They do not worship me; they mock my rites
Mechanically, in rubberized anxiety to prove
That they can probe. They probe for themselves
Among the chemicals that kill, and never find
Each other, much less me-in-them at the moment
Not-self breaks in sudden flood, which used
To reaffirm the strength, identity of me,
The goddess praised by sacrifice of self, who lived
On their dyings, aged only in those minutes when
No mortal anywhere released his urgent homage.

Now they brood and itch and breed, and read
About it—millions of them, every second—yet
Every second ages me. They no more pray in the act,
In the rote of their flesh, than they do later, when
They knock on any wood that's left. If they knew me now,
They'd collect my youth in plastic replicas, and vote
Me an old-age dole: they'd pension off the Paphian!
Perhaps they should, then let the one-time wielder
Of the world relapse into her olden, golden age.
Unthinkable—the Cypriot in corsets and blued hair!

Gone, gone are the dove-live days when love
Unwrapped the favored maidens, as a swan,
A pouchy bull, or a pocketful of shiny change.
Come are the days when people come on tick,
Or worry else, unzipping, zipping-up themselves.
It all began with that wordy thing, unworthy
Of feathers, which spoke its holy piece to the ears
Of the fidgety, fledgling virgin there, unused
To annunciations. A son was borne to die,
Knocked onto wood, all continent, aloft

In order to agonize. My doves desert
Me in my dotage. I am history. And who
At home believes me now, in me this day?
Cybele's a footnote, shells a decorator's theme,
And foam is born of detergents, or maybe of beer.

The word that voiced the unvisited womb, a word
That spread all ways but one from the sacred east,
That clad the world's last organs of prayer, and sealed
The seeds of generations in stone cells, undid me and began
This withering, these hooded eyes, dejected paps, the loins
All pinched by age (and nobody else). I'm shrunk to a name
That spurts from the slim pens of poets, or neatly fills
Five spaces in a crossword puzzle—I, the breasted one
Who templed all the knowing world: that ball which curled
To the curve of my instep: I, Venus, am grown old, alone

Of the Olympians, the last to die! I'll drink to them,
The ghosts I used to guzzle with, and bother so, on high.
I'll toast, as well, with this last tot of ancient nectar, all
My progeny, the devotees who heroed it in all my brawls,
And those dear, last few anachronists who kneel to me
Naked, on sunny shores unknowingly.
                                    I wonder: one
Last time? With whom—and could another god be got?
At my age, and the world's? I'd like to try. Could Cytherea turn
The trick of Nazareth, and leave the world a love-child thus?
I dream, and my last cup has lapsed to lees.
                                    I was.

BLOSSOMS FROM BAYEUX

Chrysanthemums on blue, with blood and sun,
Old blood, paled gold dyeing their leaves,
Loose their shocks, shake stooks to the air
Static here, like stacks of greaves (not grain)
That a bleeding soldiery limped out of overnight,
Withdrawing in autumn, all dark, and thirstily bled,
Bearing their honor unarmed through the ritual cold.

This ruined, frozen chivalry redeems our heat,
But rasps immediately on silence as we breathe
And read in light and warmth of the wild outdoors,
Of knees stone-worn through bloody tapestry to bone,
The axed-lipped leers of the carbuncled churls,
And the roseate morals misted in samite courtesy.
(Dirty, those years, and glued with blood; the sun so small.)

Bright dawnsong drawn austerely through complaint
Rubs habit square to shape Gregorian desire: so old
Is ordinance indoors, and so cold is declaration here,
That speech floods copper flowers with stale breath.
Yet flowers must weave their groping roots in the ground
Of soil so often soiled, the airy and chambered brain,
And send their beauty stiff, to collapse in a grieving season.

LORDS OF THIS EARTH:
AN ELDER SPEAKS

1.

We came at last, cold in our cabinned righteousness,
Stiff to the very codpiece with all sorts of salt
And stain, bareheaded to our virgin land, our second
Eden.
  We came to pines, to sand and supple savages
Who knew nor Christ nor modesty, whose cornhills stank
And whose women smelled, in what clothes they wore,
Like wives anywhere.
     Though warred upon and plagued
For their silly sins, yet everywhere—and outdoors too—
Noiseless under the wretched pines, warm breast brown
On heathen breast, and black polls mingled to the sky,
They couple, and Lord knows but they pup thus in the face
Of the Almighty, like the godless animals we know they are.

2.

What dross have they given back for our redeeming cross—
What return for the Word from these slippery, guttural souls?
Naught but their wild cob-corn, fish, springs, faint trails . . .
O sure our God is Lord of All, and their beastly Manitou
Offers but berries, beads and shells, mere skins against
The skills and engines, armor, clothes of our contrivance,
Books, The Book: the eternal glory of our chaste rewards.

3.

Whether these creatures kneel or flee; whether they die
In famine or fight; Our Covenant gives unto us this land:

Its beasts to our powder and shot, its fish to our wires,
Its trees to our axes and fires of steel and flint.
                                        This land
Lies all before us from the east to take and plow with prayer,
Mayhap with profit. So let the rusty dead bury—wherever—their
Unsermoned and unlessoned dead. We are here to clean and slay.

            4.
God says to seize, and so we may
Have to destroy in order to stay;
Such destruction makes us pray—
The best of us . . .
                    And yet, as regards
Those simple folk that delved and span,
Whose image was only as Nature's man,
And had not our God, but only gods—
Had they no wisdom there?
                        Oh, but I
Am an old man dazed by the spreading sky—
Forgetting Eden, forgetting the fires of Hell.

NOW THAT GOD'S GRAVE

Now that god's grave has been danced over, every inch,
For two hundred years, and deep-sealed with the blood
Of nuns raped and savaged, and soiled by satanic seed
From the couplings of humorless brothers and sisters
Spouting tumultuous verses as well, most vocal of tears—
Now that what once were just dreams (the warm, salty ones
Of dying, the hot ones of death) have come wetly true,
And nothing is left to shed on the grave, and the grave
Is not easy to find under six christslives of feet—
What can man do in the twin generations he's given,
Between sperm and sigh, blood and blood, the tearing
And tears of those left, between nothing and nothing?

Having shouted *no god*, announced *nature*, and whispered of *history*,
Stumbled man must get over his rise from the fall, and recover
From gone-away god, from gulled virgin and hoisted redeemer.
Humbled, he'll have to find, faint in his fellows, a long
Debauched divinity, now that god's gone and man's grave.

SHEM, SHAM, AND THE
SHAME OF NATIONS

The human race, newenglanders as well as old
southwhite suprematists, and the coalblue men
of the bush, will blush or bleach to the middling shade
of fate, or no one will live.

Abroad in the widest of wars, black sam,
unchained and clad in the leveling tan,
turned burning propagandist, and with just
one spark of nature's fire reduced
to glowing ruins thousands of thighs
of a smitten mistress race.

Back home the masters dreamed legree all day
and scotched themselves with flaccid whips
of rhetoric, and then in the catgraying dark
took sip of the jewel-lipped girls, while ham,
rampant, redivivus, overseas,
plied his probing irony.

The sixth of columns, in underground movement,
could spread out the flush of old shame on the face
of earth's people, make the race human,
the color of life that can last.

IN SPITE OF THINGS

Under a ceiling of yellowing islands and white
Ocean mapped out by an overflowed bathtub upstairs,
Behind a window cracked from departed anger, within
Walls streaked by the sighs of a toilet tired somewhere,
On a bedspring lyre off pitch with an ancient passion,
More love has burst to light than we can know
And kept the world moving under the stars
In spite of the city.

More music than anyone ever will hear has erupted
From fingernails pale pink with shame for the shoes
They have polished of whiteankled people, the shoes
Of the city: black, oxblood, hard yellow;
A battered piano makes music much brighter than blackness,
Shapes idols of smoke, and keeps the world living out loud
In spite of the nation.

More people than anyone ever could know in the countries,
In the soot of the noisy slums or the dust of the lonely huts,
By paddy or prairie, by pawnshop or supercanned market;
More people than anyone knows can't help laughing,
And everywhere someone is changing the somecolored baby
And keeping the world pinned together, all over
In spite of the great coalitions.

III

LEGACIES

For three American centuries
The breeding Christians let
My forebears work and walk in praise,
On Sundays don the deacons' get.

In kitchen, cubing sandwich bread
To pass with thimbles of altered wine,
My mother stood (who long ago lay in bed
Upstairs for me with that formal father of mine),

While I gave idle help to that good wife
Who's grandma now to boys I brimmed to life.

My father has always heard the deepest rhymes
        Of poetry,
         If not of me;
     And when he goes to family dirt,
     I'll follow, clothed in hugest hurt.

Staring at a thin gold watch, I'll think of times.

ON THE BASHING OF BOATERS

The stiff straw hat my father wore each day,
The city summer, the sweaty season through,
On Saturday noon before Labor Day in the front
Hall of our house, as soon as he stamped in to sigh
His windiest for us inside, then fiercely snapped
At its saucer of brim, and skimmed down the hall
To our strictly-soled, lifting feet, we jumped

On in jubilee, crushing it, jumping, and smashed
Into chaff that sailing shape, and I laughed.
Ritually, each year, for those few of my years
(My boyhood ago to my fatherhood now that I've halved
Through my children the span between boy and old man),
I with no hat who let nonsense spread through the year,
Jumped, I remember, just on that day, helping demolish

The rigid round which had stuck to my father's skull
All summer long, and held his hopes, and perhaps
His angry plans, and his dreams for the smashers he shod.
Back then we jumped out loud, and I jump in my mind to this :
Perversely crashing promises, and loudly collapsing straws.
Both fashions and families change, and I've nothing to float
Now, but my shapeless dreams for these sneakered boys to burst.

EPITHALAMION

1.

Veering alone towards evening here,
I think how many poems will be given
Or got this night, how deep will be
The verbing of the bodies everywhere,
How many strictest rhymes rung out
In the dark throat, in strong discourse
Of opposites, the antiphons of holy war.
I hear outlast all early summer nights:
Two lovers locked in dawnsong and complaint
Against the doom of day, thin edge of entering noon.

2.

Lady away from me, let me now make song,
Make love out loud in the voiceless throat
To you who knead the bread of peace
Between your thighs, and shape the sword
Of self to share; and let me try
To tell the rosary of your design.

3.

This earth of round oceans and rivers between
Green shadows, blunt mountains, dark sky,
The streamings of cloud, all the stars
Remotely attendant: this earth was allowed
Before your birth to be a trope, a sign,
And after you are gone shall grow a shrine.

       I dreamed a dream that you would bend
       Great God Himself on His huge knees to pray
       What god He could to make another one
       So witnessing His bibled powers as you.

4.

Your breasts are models Eve, alone
Of women, once made apples on, the forms
For which God, happy then, first made
The artist's two good hands: your breasts
That feed on feeding love, and fill.

And from the shadow of your breast you still
Dispense an immortality to songs
And sonnets long ago that claimed to turn
To marble flesh of ladies ages dust
That chastely mantles bone so deep below.
Alert, your crowning nipples look to me
To polarize and set this toppling world.

5.

Each part of you makes allegory past
The last scholastic's latest dream;
Large volumes of heroic verse
Lie baffled in your eyebrow's finest hair.

Even eyes like mine, in level stare,
Compound themselves in eyes of yours,
And bounce towards bent infinity until
The image echoes down to final dot.

6.

Who would not be converted, goddess, by
The suasion of such limbs, or caught
In tiny hairs that curl against the nape
Of innocence columnar, wise as yours?

Yet some at a concert of music must cough,
Or in cathedral slit their eyes to probe
His carven robes, and sculp the naked saint.

7.
The scent of just your honey hair collecting sun

Is proof that sun in season seeks a land,
And in desirous vacuum sighs the wind—
The warm wind like a bee to my desire;
The sun swarms down and yields to me
The gold of more than thirty vivid springs.

8.
Now, on the lawn relieved of afternoon,
Still alone, with you and loveliness in mind,
I watch the scimitar-shouldered swallows dare
The May. With little cries like stars they wheel
And harry dusk as though to eat of it, maneuvering
For life on evening air: too swift and proud,
Perhaps too quick upon a thirst of wind,
To braid with me my lady's vesperal hair.

9.
I praise your insouciant thighs,
Their stride and brave decisions
(Luxuriant in shadowed privacy):
Tall walking legs of yours that, strong,
Yet unlike men's, walk not behind
Their pride, but walk around their warm
And secret honor—only cause of pride.

I have gone up to die in the sacred grove
At confluence and kiss of your two rich
And ivory rivers flowing to their source.

10.
Your body, yours alone of those I know,
Or those the bare world bleats about,
Is body mind enough and clean to make
And grow these monstrances: milk-blue
Of a baby's outer eye, and the dreams
Beneath his bath-curled hair.

Your flesh
Reports its own magnificence
In generations due this waiting race.

You, tabernacle, sanctify my seed;
My seeking seed you shape to its idea:
You artist of my urge, and deity
To whom I kneel in act, but pray aloud
In words whose only use could ever be
To try to clothe, and thus in voice reveal,
My wordless, obvious love for you: a love
Recaptureless, and helpless not to die.

11.
Alone as evening dies, all swallows gone,
I weave these twigs of words for your return.

NO DAUGHTER OF MINE

The littlest person I have ever loved
And the briefest, so maybe the best I have loved
Has long lain scattered of liver and lights and fine eyes
Once bright with questions of me, but soon tired
Of the handful of hours they had already known,
Blue eyes that drew their lids to let me know
To let her go.
              That body wrongly light
Is now many years of me gone to some earth,
With no stone, as we wished it, and nothing for name.

Unfathered by nothing : no daughter of mine.

MAY HAPPEN

Breezing out among these things,
I stopped and spun, then rooted there;
Threw out my arms in bloom, and so,
Nodded with the rest to see my dear
Along the street serenely treading light
And moving for the benefit of air.

4 JULY

Suddenly it's dusk, and all overhead
The exclamation-points of light go up
And droop to us, go bang, disintegrate;
The sparks drift down like imagined snow.

As children clap and parents shift on the turf,
Another goes up with a vow and a wish, then goes off
All over us, soft as any eye could ask, till the flak-
Like banging begins that pulls up my overseas hands.

But the kids ride sleepily home without questions
In our sandy, rocketless car; then slide into dreams
That blossom enormously, quietly, into the night.

THIS PRESENCE UPSTAIRS

With the hips and short legs
of a tireless peasant, the trunk
of a child, goes Michiko's face,
burnished smooth by the war
of her childhood, and bright
by the faith which drives all her days.

She turns the same cameo-face
on our ranting, unruly young,
with their guns and ingratitude
cocked, as on their regardless
parents, whose study is gin,
and only prayer is twisting verse.

She eats our bread, and beds
with us, helps clean our dishes
and wash our clothes; her calling
takes her thus far from the fires
of her father's perishing to our
agnostic abundance, barbarous love.

THE HARDEST PARTING

(*Clarence Horace Philbrick, 1891–1959*)

1. October 30

"It is like living two parallel dreams," he told me,
In the days of medication, at noon on the day
Of my last visit. We talked of dreams, of John
Hay's genius for prose, of windows and the imminent
Arrival of my brother Tom. "Is it really that bad?"
"No, dear; it's just that he can get away this weekend,
Convenient for all, and snow will be coming," said Mother.
He glazed to the other track of glazed reality,
His last, for a moment, then turned to realize me
Again in the heated room. His voice stumbled out
From the dry, drained, shut-off cave of his body,
Flapping up through sucked-in lips in his tapped,
Collapsing face: body both bloated and shrunk: cool,
Thin right arm dropped out and free from the tubes
In greeting and goodbye to take my hand, which felt
Huge, red and hot, almost indecently alive up there.

2. The First Week in November

I have November deep in me now,
Since I have seen what I have seen;
And yesterday wrestles under the pillow while
Tomorrows warren under our patriarchal bed.

Those unaware are limp upstairs, one here
In a top bunk, one down in a crib, and there,
And there—all nestling soft their unimaginable fill
Of skulls so intricately downed. They've heard
Of death, and maybe dream of it, heroically—
Two months make visitors' footsteps on my marrow,
Whispering along the pith of my unbroken bones.

One hundred miles away
From this slow-pulsing bay,
The hordes of horror swarm
That body, brangling through
The blood that, my life ago, surged
In another, my mother, to make me be.
There he lies, as his mother lay
When I was a boy the age of my first son—
As I may lie when he has reached my age,
And can likewise feel three deaths in one.

3. November 14

My father's body became its earth
In a doctor's wonder: his quiet refusal
To die for a week after bodies have to die.
Three days before he lost his body's fight,
They pulled all plastic tubes for other use,
And left him to his slack and poisoned blood.
Oxygen they took away, as well as bottled food
And all pale veins that made his circulation.
Then his skyless eyes loomed to their ceiling,
And scummed like city windows on the prison
Of his restless, unattended brain.

He achieved a coma while Mother was there,
In her wren-inspecting presence, then came back
To try it again without painkiller, pipes or mask,
Or even the pipping pulse, then, supposedly dead,
Said to her clearly, "Mary."
                           Not query or cry, I think,
But a statement of *Mary* to Mother all breasted in love,
Half-ghosted in her untouchable grief.
                                 The problem then:

To stop that sullied blood, and quiet that fierce heart,
Those uninvaded lungs: to let that old man die, and teach
To die post-operative and walking people such as I.

      IV. November 28, and Thereafter
Now we sketch a stone to sit in the turf
His ashes shall inherit, and we plan
What shrubs we hope will gird the rock
Whose incised name we open to every air.

These words are name and date, and little more
Than that but clinical detail: cut epigraph, but no
Enlarging elegy on him who gifted us with life
As well as grief. Such praise is inward still,
Though memory may moss the edge of stone,
And ivy it all in a love too long kept locked
As in a rock. But even now in spare remembrances,
Agreeing on celebrations and the care of graves,
We walk in indulgent suns of his laughter,
      among the stones of his deeds.

TWO RELEASES (1945, 1959)

Richard, younger brother, halfway down our dead father's years,
Whose memory we churched today, all in dress, by the flowers,
With well-mouthed words skewing at us and over in scent as we sat
Up close in the foremost, pitiless pews, with our properly brave,
Softly indecisive mother beside us under the organ's bleached,
Mild meanderings that laved the dome with comfort until
The Right Things and the things not wholly wrong were said:
Richard, bearing so many of that dead man's cares, do you remember
Now your own much less private lying in a makeshift hospital's bed?

You were flown back to England, stacked alive to lie separate in pain,
With other young men up-arched in hurt dying around you, while older,
Also sweating men in white dug most of the jagged seeds of your
      death
From your marrow-sapped, desperately young, spent body. All but
      the heel
They cleaned in that barracks and shambles, of you who, underage,
Made it across the Remagen Bridge, and were birthdayed there on
      the far
Side by sudden mortarfire from a firred ridge on the German Rhine;
Thereafter struggling up to command, and then not to fall:
Last leader of a first platoon into that war's last hell.

Your bed, that spring, was kindled by shrapnel sparking your body.
Now, just this autumn, we've watched a cool bed, all lukewarm-tubed
To a cooling body, cleaned outside, but all dark battle within,
While the lapping mind glazed its shores against unknown winters
Of eternity, certain at least that his enemies there were encircled
In their merited levels of shrill unwit and steep orbits of denial.

Just because, Dick, this good man has gone difficult, gray from us,
We must go all our days left in spending remembered good, go gray
Ourselves as slowly and only outside of us as we can, and be gay
As seems easy among the weedy brains that sketch our paths, and milk
Themselves of their stale poison as we pass.
                                        That man whose mind
Presides on all our memories: his courage flecked on your reluctant
Bones, his myths and laughter plucking every word I try to live upon:
He lived, our father, hard in his way, and strong with the strength
Of all his fathers, and stronger against their legacied strength.

Weeks past the date he left the lighted place, and became both himself
And his ashes—not ours any more, or theirs of ancestral morality,
Or even worried Mother's in all her devotion, but just his best
Sinew of singular spirit, rare in the black Alone.
                                        At longest last
He went quietly elsewhere, out of his ruined, our-life-giving body,
And went not at all to the pastelled rewards of pink, palm and pearl,
In his kept and diaconal cutaway, but naked and wrecked, up high,
Into the cloud of his crowding recognitions, probably laughing.

IV

RESURRECTION IN THE NEIGHBORHOOD

Our black and witless dog digs dawn at Easter out
Of a hillside in the park-becoming-dump across our street.
What paschal bone, we window-wonder, scares he there?
What buried Easter urges on his paws? And in the dirt
He digs so fast and backward flings at the low sun,
Lurks what winterslept and toadly smiling soil of sin,
That this dawndrunk and springstruck delver, furious,
Should be so wide avoided by the pairs of glossy feet,
So shunned by those who leg it first to earliest Mass?

They, of course, the shaven-shining, florist-fresh,
In their brisk of piety and smoothly vested flesh,
Had no idea, nor did that small, black, unfed dog,
Rampaging in the scrawny wood, inspired to dig,
Nor we who idled nearly naked at the curtain, then,
That it would snow all Easter morning, that the sun
Would shrink to farthest paten, while the earth, that pale
Unleavened host, would freeze again, or that the grail
I'd raise to all of them is brimmed with seep of brain,
With sap and spurt of Spring, and other-bloodless wine.

SPRINGS

On a tricycle left in marbletime (in Town,
In Spring), the curbside maples drop slow smiles
Of blossom, sluice the gutters bright. The drift
Of this greengold treemoulting veins the asphalt,
Warming all black decency, adopting all abandoned toys.

Over the river from pavement, and under the bent
Exclamation of blue, in the brandnew dump,
The tincans wink like water at the sun.
Beyond, in the dip, in the lack of land and gap
Of house, the peepfrogs stretch their green and yell
And try to chug, just spoiling for their Spring.

In Park across the Town, the breeze which cups
A gentle compress of cool Sunday skirt
Against the buttocks of the tall young girls
(Who did not walk so carefully last Spring),
Halfway heals what did not hurt last Spring.
Slow in doublebreasted suits young men
Pomaded, promenade and grant to grass
The popcornbags uncrumpling into bloom
Behind their feet. Their eyes play breeze
With slippery knees; they seem to know somehow
That someday something Spring will come to pass.

Out of Town, past the dump, and away from Spring,
And the circling Park and the pavement, near
The fireplaces yet unwarmed, a bulge
Of new skunk cabbage darkly speculates
On LADIES (ladies!) in the privyshade.

WHAT'S LEFT OF THE YEAR

Locust-whine saws half the summer down,
All August afternoon. The goldenrod rusts,
As old-eyed turtles cross the road by day,
And falling stars inscribe the sky by night.

Man-shadow, on September afternoons,
Stalks like a fear across the bright grass,
Where hornets weave a nest of level sun,
And whirl a yellow bowl of wine till dark.

Off in the river-watching wood the crows
Caucus on evening chill, and beak the air.
The squirreled, reluctant oaks dry slowly;
Elms make perfect fountains of their going.

Fiercely children decry the dusk and smoke
Of leaves and the year, and run October down.
November feels the sun leaning south away;
December brightly brings the littlest day.

TERRA RECOGNITA

The big-bouldered mesas and marshlands of cloud over there in the sky
We explore from our couches of grass which protest us in exquisite
    odor;
We widen our voyaging eyes to new-found land uncharted in air,
To a land where no foot falls, no roads are incisioned, and nothing to
    eat
Can be grown, to a country the flags of possession can never harpoon.

But these myths which we frond the fine air with from hummock
    towards white Himalayas
In sky are forgiven and cancelled; we see that the land which we
    thought
We discovered is already taken, is prowled and bestrode all around
By an eminence, insect prepulsed, by an airplane whose trespass of
    noise
We forgive, since we slicked with aluminum skin that taut oblongata.

Now it twists to a homing; the continent starts to erode in red air
Of the evening. The querulous trickle of sound from invisible airplane
Dies seeking our earth, and we rise from the grass to go where we
    belong.

SEAS OVER

When the full moon decides to rise and decree
A low tide trolled from every dispeopling shore,
The lolloping sea meets itself in the middle,
And tosses into fitful metaphors, far away
From the faceless lovers who lie all alone
On the moon-stretched strand, and are drawn
Up together towards that high mirroring myth
Quicksilvered with love by the lovers' race.
Silent superbly, the moon stares not to say
That their love is in thrall to her fickle shape,
That the tides of their birth are in train of her, too,
That her sea's pulse primes the pumps of their hearts,
Or that their hot heart-surges tinily mock, their hugest
Urges imitate, her ageless ministration of our seas.

KENNINGS OF PRAISE

Shelf over shellfish, foundation waves,
Greenhouse for seaweed and larder for terns,
Boat-floor and trapdoor for bodies of boatmen,
Skylighted ceiling for boat-handlers' prey,
Old innocent house of cold birth, quiet ruin:

Palette for whitecaps to clot with stiff foam,
Stippler of sun-glints and canvas for moonstroke,
Wood-wearer, stone-roller, sparer of shells,
Sand-scroller, rock-draper, sculptor of cliffs,
Orchestra spread for the wind, and metrist of weather:

This easy sea that breeds and beggars epithets,
This water that always remembers, invents and forgets.

OVERRULED

The long-lulled serpents uncoil in the pit of the brain
Of a man all alone in his house on a midsummer midnight;
Thick darkness is split by the bolt of his frightful desire,
And the heavy-set silence shakes to his thundering summons.

The roof of his skull and the walls of his house all pulse
And swell to contain his writhing demand for some other;
He feels like a coal-holding fist in a fist, as he sinks
In his clasping, soft chair. He can hear himself breathing.

Something sudden outside, a crack in the high dome of night,
Bellows an answer back, striking at earth, then releases
Huge rain. The man in the empty house moves, aims a bottle
Straight at his mouth, and fires a slow shot to the brain.

Commotion comes now all around him, no longer inside.
He is no more alone in his thrashing: a much louder lust
Beats his little snakes down. So, launched from his chair,
He plunges the house, shutting windows against the storm.

WALKING AND WOUNDED

As I walked through the city of dying elms,
    In the country of dead ideas,
Down the long streets of no destination,
    Past the people without any eyes,

I kicked at the leaves that had fallen before me,
    With angry, thick shoes,
And I pitied the great-footed strugglers above me,
    So slowly drooping to lose.

As I walked through the crowds of no neighbors,
    In my city that covers all earth,
I asked each sick tree for some answer
    To what all my walking was worth.

What sifted down with the shrunken leaves
    I thought I could almost hear,
So I walked a little more softly then:
    Where I was going was near.

A CITY AWAY

Five wild swans alone
On the dark unfrozen water
Stared it stiff round them to white.

Receiving an urchin committee
Of scrawny black duck to their pool,
The five white swans, in ermine sympathy,
Looked cold and clan-orange to their beaks.

The warm train I was in at the window drew
Its noise along towards Mystic and the City,
While I sat, glassed as a fool in wonder,
Sped by envy and issuing tickets of pity,
Or something, for five preened swans unseen.

So I seem an accident against the glass of vision,
Like five wild eye-proof swans adrift on the water,
Paddling to keep the melt their size.
                              And my eyes,
Like goldfish-bowls, englobe as in glass
Five tiny swans in shaken snow,
As trains go where I asked to go.

V

PAYING TO LAUGH

It smells like boyhood, readymade, remade.

Clowns rinse the dust of saws below
With laughter greasing back and forth
Between the paint and purchase. See
The floury cheeks, the eyebrows ascertained.

Hear the music, yellow and red,
And swing the ladies overhead;
Bar the baited animals,
And jig those jerky comicals,

Those clowns all clothed in air.
Their noses make their faces sad;
We paint the face of nothing with this blood,
This dribbling blood, and the rings all around.

It looks like history, but feels more like forever.

MADAM AMELIA'S MESSAGE

"Lost nature restored," she promised:
Madam Amelia, the Florida palmist,
On her fold-faded card of salmon—
Black Mammy and madam of Mammon.
"No problem too great for this medium,"
She claimed as she clawed at my tedium,
Asserting "no supernatural powers"
To salvage all my shipwrecked hours.
What nature that I've lost can she restore?
My infant innocence? My squandered seed?
My seed of purpose, deeply channeled, or
All the beasts dead since we Did the Deed?
"Later may be too late," Madam Amelia warns;
And at my temples I feel the regression of horns.

YOUNG COUPLE WITH KEY

In the wealthy inlaws' weekend-
  Cottage kitchen by the shore
  (Bright with copper-bottomed pans),
Hangs the trophy: tight, albino,
  Shining, brindle-haired or -rooted
Scrotum of the garden's garlic,
  Waiting for the family's guests.

After their delightful weekend,
  Newly wedded two go home;
Leave the kitchen still more tidy,
  Half the garlic on the wall.

SEEKING AND SOUGHT

The tee-shirted pervert lurks in the covert,
Alert to drop levis for look-see of girls;

The kids in the park circle locust and privet,
Scrub-oak and ivy, the brambles downhill;

They look for and scream at unspotted
That white gleam Director has damned;

While police in their cars, unmolested,
Go largely around on peripheral streets.

To the cops all kids are a bother, the park
An area rife with complaints after dark—

The whole thing a bore unless queer's caught to beat.

Now the quarry slides, scurries, then strolls,
While desire and fright alternate in his feet,
And a leaf in his fist is forgotten, and curls.

PUT-OUT

By two of the ten thick thumbs
Of a hoarse-mouthed, implacable fan
In the stands at an underattended
Ladies' Day game between teams
Both deep in the second division
At dusk in the extra fool innings
Just as the light-banks were loath
To go on, the peanut was clutched;

Just then, as the fan in the wrinkled pants
Looked up to follow the arc of a fly-out—
The pellet that mooned it a moment and sank
Into the sweat-leathered palm of a pro from
Ineffable, Arkansas, clean off the bat of
A youth from Ontology, Texas—just then,

The peanut-rind gave, as the boob and the goober came blind
To this breaking of shell, whose brief smoke shapes a question:
Could soul be a peanut, a god be all thumbs? And could body
Be husk, a dry hoax, as here in this late-season rooting?

FRIDAY NIGHT FIGHTS

Jigging, pomaded, berobed, with shoelaces whiter than white
For the camera, waving and lighthousing grins to the crowd,
The clubfighters turn from their corners fast and touch their fat gloves.
Sweatshined they spar, shifty-legged, in more than bright light;
Their muscles uncoil from their darkness; their hair flies apart to
      the loud
Fists thudding between the commercials, the clinches that mock all
      the advertized loves.
Then one of them looks up and leans back slowly and cleanly to fall,
While the other shrugs money all over, drops hands, and that's all.

A CORPSE FOR THE CARRIAGE TRADE

All of a sudden the decent trash
Pushed up at me something horrid,
Shining, real, and dead-looking: *rat*.
—Recognized rat stacked on the packaging
Gathered outside squeegeed windows, in front
Of the negligees, monogrammed silks, and forced ivy.

All of a sudden as I,
Filling an overcoat into the wind
Of winter walked by, my eye flicked this thing
So sheeny and dark, and so dead, which said to me
Ten paces later, my god, they're alive by the hundreds
If this one is dead, flounced by a car as he roamed from the river.

As I tried to rub from my mind
The image of this foot-ball fat and purpling thing
With a tapered supple tail, I wondered how such
Innocent evil—luckily dead—could survive in a cluster
Of bricked facades with aluminum edgings which squeeze
Out the cold, which must be to rats the last of resorts
On a freezing night; I wondered how all this could be.

Then I remembered slick swarms on the bank
Of the sewered and mill-muddied river, began
To feel sorry for rats in a city, desperately toothing
Cement everywhere. Then I thought of the babies whose faces
Have fattened such rats in a thousand city backyards, and looked
For a stout stick, but found none. I strode along quicker—
All children behind me—determined to call
A city official, and threaten to publicly die,
Unless the big city could pluck this lone rat from my eye.

A BARD FOR THE BIRDS

(Shelley for English Majors)

The Suntreader stumbles in English Thirty-one
(Section One); high landscapes of his mind
Are strewn with juniors' cold, stiff brains,
While senior to senior smiles at his staring moons,
Having stained his clouds with their dribbling dreams.

Can skylark soar past vacant caves of gape
And foreheads that grind on *Agapé*? Can flesh
That twitches for tweed (and mainly under it)
Arise from dreams of thee? Alastor's name
Adorn an office-door, and Adonais weep?

Prometheus will hold shrewd Asia's hand,
And Demogorgon dun for next instalment,
While Jupiter drifts from throne to throne;
The whole class waits through Shelley (lyric liar),
And annotates my homage, known till nearly June.

O, breed, you bulbs, despite your education,
Which helped you make the Dionysiac dull—
Go marry, mar and measure *your* desires:
Your odes shall be inked on disposable diapers; your sins
Unrecorded, your thoughts unforgiven; your wives shall have twins.

VI

BY APPOINTMENT

My royal blood in a mason jar amazes me
In its ready, rapid bulk, and makes me proud
That so much of me so casually can flow
So darkly red, so thick and bubbling rich
From the skinny arm I use to hold a book,
The ruined elbow that brings my drink to me.

Why should I be proud of this *purée*, at sight
Of it out of me, salt in its settling self?
I've quarts of it left for every pint I seep
Through plastic tube to chemical abuse and cold
For others' good; hot gallons I've shed in my heart,
And let a drop spread bright against each eye.

I am suddenly sick, in my health, of all blood
And the past: the impromptu clinics in tents,
The bloody runs on the future under the skies.
But all things clot in time, and some heal;
As colors fade, most poems drip away, word
By forgettable word, to form the scab
                         we scratch, and find absurd.

VISITING PRIVILEGES

First the half-grinning turnkey for visitors, then
The hard gray walls and the sliced tin cans for butts,
And the windows with the thick-painted bars
And ragged screens to discourage the flies:
The eumenides here seem listless, with nowhere to go.

Television asks the whole ward in to the idiocy
Of the shadows it shows in its pale daylit face.
Overhead an airplane unravels its homing, lazily,
While the sane prisoners' corn grows dusty, tall,
Outside in the unguarded sun. Even here it is hot.

Somebody laughing forgets how to stop till he sobs
On the shoulder of the cigarette-pocked settee.
I sit carefully, smoking reticence, close beside
My friend in clean jeans with the turned-in eyes.
When he looks up to speak (my friend), I spill
My ashes on the mopped and modern floor.
My wristwatch screams on its sweaty strap
That visiting privileges end at four.
After trouble finding his hand, I rise at last,
And the new turnkey lets me out, alone.

NIGHTWATCH: A SPECULATION

I was terribly tired of crosses when I saw
Off to the side, ten feet away, that robe
(I had been reading that poems are buried
Liturgies and creeds)—that robe that stood
Near the table in the other room, and spoke
No word until I spoke.
                 Are you real? I asked,
My invention, or my discovery? and who?

The voice in the robe rose slowly to these words:
I am only whom you know; and who can be known,
And still be real? And how could you, you man
Of words, discover me, since I've been here
Always, and elsewhere all the time? No time
Or place surrounds the landfall of my rock.

I did not dare put lip to drink, though drink
Stood on my other side; the visioned voice
Went on.
        Of course, he said, *you invented me—*
And that's the hell of heaven: every man
On earth is doomed to this: inventing me
For himself, all over again: every man.

Then the robe began to fade, and the voice
Grew paler than white:
                Maybe you'll see me again,
Who sees only you and the rest of the seeking men.

It was over before my left hand found the drink
Long poured. I drank it all, then wanted to run
Through the house and shout:
                Jesus! You should have been there!

LOBSTERS AND GIN

Why can't all people live like the live great man—
Live despite, great because—the kind man I met
This summer who's known all those people and places
And times, and spun out all those poems that pluck
At the sensitive ear, and those other dark songs
That anchor fast under the shift and flow of the slick
On the reading-full mind?
                                        O other eldering men,
Why have you put away all those canaries, brought home—
Accoladed, bifocalled and raised unto suburbs—the world's
Rancid bacon,
While Conrad Aiken
Can roll from his garden and quietly rollick,
Encouraging me? The answer is simple: we live on the fringes,
Desperately,
On lobsters and gin, and the thunder of unbuyable verse.

BARN IN JULY

Sawdust and sweat. Heat behind windows of webs.
Fly-whine over the curls of freed wood.
The burls and the grains, the whorls and gnarls
Of every slice-taking, odorous, workable
Wood. And where it rounds easy or hard:

The polish on knobs, the shine on the edges
Of tools held hard on the palm, held steady
To wetted, wheeling whetstones, then ready
For dangerous trial in grainy-grimed cuttings
On squared wood, seasoned, sawn from tall trees.

Angling and curving, itching and learning,
Hot in unlimited afternoon: the artificer,
Half-past thirteen, finds the give and the hate,
The moods of materials, the weakness or whim
Of each tool, whether dusty or bright. And evening

Can never come, nor any summer die while he,
Thirteen for always, shapes and hones himself despite
His hunger and sweat that sparks on his eyes,
The stiffening blood at the heel of one punished thumb.
In the hot, hand-hewn barn, put together with tapering pegs,

In school out of school, out of earshot he works,
Crafting his manhood alone, as though young
Could get old, or the red sun finally die
On the burliest apple-tree west of the barn,
And the thing made of wood could be finished,
                              imperfect forever.

A PILLAR OF SMOKE: THE FIRST DAY

The first day I saw such smoke
(Lamenting my edge on an act of war),
It rose through the clouds from my grandmother's town—
The seat of the Nürnberg stove—
And nothing came up to contest our view.

The last day I saw such a dark crown of fire
(Preluding cessation of war),
Was some miles away when an airplaned friend of mine
Seized a stone barn with his burning machine,
And gave the war up all at once. That was his last
Mission flown before homing; his last flight brought him down.

I have been back here a long time since then,
And read so many photographs of smoke
(So much higher, shaped of such fatter hate),
That it must be trivial to sit down and think
Of the leisurely, shifting pillar of smoke
That climbed from my grandmother's harmless old town,
Those wars and a third of this life ago, that first of the days.

THE HAND

My vainglory once, this collection of carrots
Unbunching away from my uprooted wrist;
Subtle they used to be, supple and strong
In their deeds, the despair of the heaviest hoof.

These fingers have dreamed over orchestra-ed blossoms,
While holding the pipeweed alone, and have guided
The opening rose, and modelled such gourds
As guerdon all virgins for godhead in renaissance paint.
These fingers have winnowed the dream from the tendrils
On a head which Rossetti would slum through Heaven for.

Hand, you have held a nervous tiller hard
To helm a craft home in air that was heavy
Or quick, the first home for the pennant.

Hand, you have teased and commanded, and driven
An airplane through whirlwinds and shallows of sky—
The man-clouded, metal-flecked, necessary air,

Thereon drawn arabesques in vapor, sent
Therethrough the suited self straight hurtling down
Until your finger, growing wart for guilt,
Released the seed of the skinned and trembling wings.

You pulled and twisted all away to safety.
                                        Instrument,
You splay your agents on these lettering keys,
Or pinch pen, charcoal, pencil or the brush
Which hoped to put your possibilities on paper.
You have fondled unto blood the lovely knife,
Alive on its clean slim own, seeking the shape
That curls inside the squared and wrinkling wood.

In your grasp a foot or two from my brain
Have shaken a cold round glass and a hot square gun.
You have tried to cup dust, and directed your fingers
Into the damp and indifferent earth.
                              Puppets
        Have lived on your fingers, and flowers have died
        In their closing. Children allow you to gloss them,
        Caress and correct them—have given you hands.

    And so dream,

Poor grown-upon palm, of your history halfway,
Before you pucker to nothing or swell to no skill.
You hand of mine, do not forget all your handling;
Remember to thrust yourself, all apt and open, up from the dark,
Through the earth laid upon me by hands of the others, and join
Polydactyllic grass on the floor of the sky to grope for the sun.

ABOUT THE AUTHOR

There he sits by the window, looking alone.
Thirty-five years ago he was born in this city.
(That makes him older than Owen or Keats; older
Than Marlowe and Shelley, when death got hold of their tongues;
The senior of Sidney, and maybe of Villon;
He has more than the years of Hart Crane when that poet
Fierce in the dark took his element's last embrace.)
Having gone to the local schools, and the general war,
He is married, and most in his circle agree that they like
And envy him his tall, exciting wife.
(He writes about her half the time; the rest
Of the time . . .) Four sons they have; the names of these lads
—But here we must end; he has already started to speak
As we have come near him. Let us hear him now.

. . . also the words, always the words of things,
Long before I dreamed my wife and children,
Back when summer was the longest season possible;
When in my fledgling head first flew all flight
Of birds imaginable, and every wind, and most
The wind southwest and up an empty hill
In the sun all afternoon all summer long.
Pulsing my skull as well were somehow drums
And violets, the boiling clouds, wild grapes,
And hero me out loud in virgin woods.

Far off: the wrath so cold and moral of the waves
At gull-caprice; sealavender and tarry rope;
The stonewall poison-ivy, birchbark, knives,
Pistolgrips and woodcurls, leather, warm
Stones to hold the other side of dunes;
Dark places, flame, and being sad

Alone, and private bright resolve.
                                        I see
Upstairs through the door the boy in the bathtub
—Grotto of adolescence—: there the shadow
On his waving body underwater: hair
Of me so secret, wanted, water-flourishing
And black.
                    I feel the scorn from every mirror,
Shame again that reeked through overlighted
Rooms perfumed with heat.
                                        No longer then
A public voice for song, but the late and long
Nights of Keats unheard in the singing bed.

In nineteen-thirty-five, in the frozen year
Of apple men at the trolley-tunnel hoarse
As pity, unconditionally cold, and older
With cold, shining their apples to the gloss of a curse,
I was a boy out of knickers barely: years
Of brief summers then, and a different school
In the winter, school of the wouldn't-be poor.

Next the candles by the dozens frame
The darkness of the Mass, the compassed chaos
Whence eternity erupts, and light:
A liturgy of light, a creed of knees:
The painsweet guided fall of anguish drawn
Through Palestrina's voices. Churchèd God
Who strains His wine through violins, and eats
The bread of brightness, God Who visits me
As dazzle in the eyes, Who comes to pass
A hand all incense over faces, bursts
In ears as music, truth on tongue, and as
The Act of Art on choirèd throats, is Deity

Of kneeling young enough in midnight church
In sanctifying clothes, up-late elect
—But never again that making God the same
As in the first full public braindeaf mouthing of
                              His Name.

We boys, perhaps exulting over croaks just gone,
In the teens of our time, late thirties of the age,
In summer took youth neat, outdoors, with wind
For a chaser. Then we ran, and stopped to throw,
Swam, sailed and raced, grew wise in our ways
In the spindrift stiffening our eyes, and cooled
Our sunstrong throats with careless beer. Our print
Was on the things of these words:
                              a stone, saltwhited,
Thrown hard against the sky, a gambling tiller,
The repertoire of terns, and the sheer of hulls
At anchor on the tide laid level by the sun.
The summers had grown long again before the war.

I can't but recall in my hair the press and form
Of fear as clutching leather helmet, hear
Death's tiny resonance at aching ear,
Or feel the thumbs of microphone at throat
In case of who knew what.
                              And I have seen
A fine man fire a slope and spend his rich
Machine to splash his quarter-century
Of zeal on nobody's hill somewhere, while I,
Anxious of fuel and possibly safe, turned back
So full of blood, and lapping over in
My brain the pearl to be, plus me,
My bright friend John, or else no war was ever won.

The diction—level, clipped, dispassionate—
Of my six guns discoursing strictly from
My stiffened wings, outshoots the static
Bristle of my voice on wireless even now.
Some button—"bomb" or "radio" or "gun"—got stuck,
Pushed in too hard on my gloved and fisted brain,
Then, more than a decade gone.

                And all we left
Beside our quick and dead, was contrails there:
Brief emanations in the air of our
High sweat and icy purpose; left our blood,
Unless it rains a little pink on Europe
Still; no mind, but memory put safe away
In dreams as old today as bad.

                      Our peace
Can only be forgotten war, the streams
Dissolving, leaking brilliance in the sky.

After war, and stranger than before,
There were the blinding books, the poems assigned;
While sex was still elective, love required
Its own curriculum. So proudly we,
As though we were the only ones, made love,
Made children, made a home in which the future
Drags itself late upstairs each night to bed.

We who've climbed the sacred mount know well
How God delighted in creating hills,
How apples start in children's cheeks, not trees,
And how the heart of everything is in
Exchange and not possession.

                  On your hip
You wear the hand I left there like a trophy
Brought from war, and from my cupping palm

I must pluck your breast before I grip
The outstretched world that others us around.

Our knowledge can be stated small: *create*
Means *will, then fill, a void which makes all whole.*
We have stamped these names on the years coming in:
Stephen, Timothy, Benjamin, Harry.
                              These names,
                    Words,
          Syllables,
Sounds,
          And so much to do. . . .

Thus our man who makes his living teaching
Other people's children at this college
In the city of his birth, and all his grandparents' death.
Perhaps the city of our poet's mind, indeed,
In a very real sense extends beyond
The boundaries of his begetting, so to speak
(One feels that such alliteration might
Receive indulgence of the poet's ear);
Further, we must insist that his life, despite
His happy marriage, plain fidelity,
Drab occupation, lack of flair in the eyes
Of either fame or scandal, is, in its way,
And to the finer eye of scholarship, no less
Exciting than the life of Shelley, and no more
Restricted than the life of Keats; Hart Crane
Accepted less responsibility;
Villon still less, while Marlowe, Sidney, Owen
Got their glories from the bloody hands
Of strangers, died in prime and promise, and away
From home.
          But this, we suppose, is "American Grain":

One can die in one's dooryard, live in school, and one
Can lie exiled in the bed of birth.
—But enough of generalization. Here
Is a middle-aged poet in mid-career;
No wreath of our approval on his brow,
He sits while we listen.
                              Perhaps we can use, we know,
This news of his musing, if—where did he go?

A LIP ON OLIVANT

Like
Roland
All arranged
For death at Roncesvalles
The horn full wound, all else undone
In the cold pass now stiffening with legendary bones
Long towards the north in a white *haleine* at last
As the dark comes down with the closest steel
In the forlorn gully at dusk, more loud
Than any *réveillés* bright chivalry
Could ever draw—
                           I call
To death
            like Roland all arranged
                              and call again.